Temporary Assistance for Needy Families: Welfare Waivers

Gene Falk
Specialist in Social Policy

September 21, 2012

Congressional Research Service

7-5700

www.crs.gov

R42627

CRS Report for Congress

Prepared for Members and Committees of Congress

Summary

The Department of Health and Human Services (HHS) announced that it is willing to waive certain federal work participation standards under the Temporary Assistance for Needy Families (TANF) block grant to permit states to experiment with "alternative and innovative strategies, policies, and procedures that are designed to improve employment outcomes for needy families." The major provision that HHS would waive is the numerical performance standards that states must meet or risk being penalized through a reduction in their TANF block grant. HHS announced this initiative on July 12, 2012.

The TANF statute provides that 50% of all families and 90% of two-parent families included in a participation rate are required to be engaged in work, though few states have ever faced the full standard because this percentage is reduced for certain credits. For all years from FY2002 through FY2006 and in FY2008 and FY2009, the majority of states had an effective (after-credit) TANF work participation standard of 25% or less. In FY2009, 22 states had their 50% all family standard reduced to 0% because of these credits. Additionally, many states have avoided the two-parent standard altogether by assisting that portion of their caseload with state funds not subject to TANF work standards.

To be considered engaged in work under the TANF standard, a family must either be working or in specified welfare-to-work activities for a minimum number of hours per week. Pre-employment activities such as job search, rehabilitative activities, and education count for a limited period of time or under limited circumstances. Though these counting rules do not apply directly to individual recipients, they may influence how a state designs its welfare-to-work program. States that allow participation in activities that cannot be counted (e.g., job search or education in excess of their limits) do not receive credit for that participation and potentially risk failing the work standard.

The new waivers would permit states to have welfare-to-work initiatives assessed using different measures than the TANF work participation rate. Thus, states could test alternative welfare-to-work approaches by engaging recipients in activities currently not countable without risk of losing block grant funds. States would have to apply for waivers, which must be approved by HHS and the Office of Management and Budget (OMB). States would also be required to monitor performance measures and evaluate the alternative welfare-to-work program. HHS also indicated it might waive some requirements that apply to states for verifying work activities.

The Government Accountability Office (GAO) has determined that the waiver initiative constitutes a "rule," subject to the Congressional Review Act (CRA). Under the CRA, if a "resolution of disapproval" is passed by Congress and signed by the President (or the President's veto is overridden), the waiver initiative could not take effect. On September 20, 2012, the House passed such a "resolution of disapproval" (H.J.Res. 118) of the waiver initiative.

The legislative authority cited by HHS to grant waivers in public assistance programs dates back to 1962, although the new initiative would allow the first new waivers to test welfare-to-work strategies in more than 15 years. "Waivers" have historically been important in welfare reform, and TANF let states continue their pre-1996 waivers until their expiration. The last such waiver expired in 2007.

Contents

Figures

Tables

Appendixes

Contacts

Introduction

The Department of Health and Human Services (HHS) announced that it is willing to waive certain federal work participation standards under the Temporary Assistance for Needy Families (TANF) block grant to permit states to experiment with "alternative and innovative strategies, policies, and procedures that are designed to improve employment outcomes for needy families." The work participation standards are numerical performance standards that each state must meet or risk being penalized through a reduction in its block grant. These are standards that apply to the states, not directly to individuals, though they may influence how states design their welfare-to-work programs.

Such waivers will be the first "new" waivers to test welfare-to-work strategies in more than 15 years. The waiver initiative would permit states that undertake an alternative welfare-to-work strategy to assess their programs using measures different from those in the current standards. HHS announced this policy through the release of an Information Memorandum on July 12, 2012.[1] State requests for waivers will have to be approved by HHS and the Office of Management and Budget (OMB), and meet specified criteria.

Under the 1996 law that created TANF, states had the authority to operate programs created under waivers of pre-1996 welfare law until their scheduled expiration. The last such waiver expired in 2007. Additionally, the Administration of President George W. Bush made a legislative proposal to create new "superwaiver" authority that would, among other things, have allowed for the waiver of the federal TANF work participation standards. That proposal passed the House three times between 2002 and 2005. A scaled-back version of this proposal was reported from the Senate Finance Committee, but not approved by the full Senate, twice during that period.

This report discusses

- the current TANF work participation standards;

- the HHS initiative to waive TANF work participation standards;

- pre-1996 welfare waivers, including how they were treated under TANF; and

- the "superwaiver" proposal.

This report is not a legal analysis of the Secretary's authority to waive TANF work participation standards. Rather, it describes and provides context for this HHS initiative.

TANF and Its Work Participation Standards

TANF is a broad-based block grant that provides funds to states, the territories, and Indian tribes to help them finance cash welfare programs for needy families with children as well as provide a wide range of other benefits and services to either ameliorate the effects of, or address the root

---

[1] U.S. Department of Health and Human Services, Administration for Children and Families, Office of Family Assistance, *Guidance Concerning Waiver and Expenditure Authority Under Section 1115*, Information Memorandum, TANF-ACF-IM-2012-03, July 12, 2012, http://www.acf.hhs.gov/programs/ofa/policy/im-ofa/2012/im201203/im201203.html.

causes of, child poverty. The basic federal block grant for the 50 states and the District of Columbia is funded at a total of $16.5 billion per year. States are required, under a provision known as the maintenance of effort (MOE) requirement, to expend from their own funds a minimum total of $10.4 billion per year in addition to federal funds on TANF or TANF-related programs.

The statutory purpose of TANF is increasing state flexibility to achieve goals to

1. provide assistance to needy families so that children may be cared for in their own homes or in the homes of relatives;

2. end the dependence of needy parents on government benefits by promoting job preparation, work, and marriage;

3. prevent and reduce the incidence of out-of-wedlock pregnancies and establish annual numerical goals for preventing and reducing the incidence of these pregnancies; and

4. encourage the formation and maintenance of two-parent families.

States may use TANF funds to finance any activity "reasonably calculated" to achieve these four TANF goals. This gives states broad leeway in spending TANF funds. In general, state MOE funds can be used for these same activities (there are some technical differences in the use of federal and state funds). Cash welfare itself accounted for less than 30% of all TANF and MOE funds in FY2011.

TANF provides states with a great deal of flexibility in designing their cash assistance programs. However, there are federal standards and requirements that apply to states with respect to providing cash assistance, including time limits and work participation standards.

The TANF Work Participation Standards

TANF sets minimum work participation standards that a state must meet. The standards are performance measures computed in the aggregate for each state, which require that a specified percentage of families be considered engaged in specified activities for a minimum number of hours.[2] A state that fails to meet its work standard is at risk of being penalized through a reduction in its block grant.

The TANF statute provides that 50% of all families and 90% of two-parent families included in the participation rate are required to be engaged in work. However, as discussed in detail below, few states have ever faced this standard because the percentage is reduced for caseload reduction or state spending in excess of what is required under the TANF MOE. Additionally, not all families receiving cash assistance are included in the participation rate calculation, as some families do not have a "work-eligible" individual or are otherwise disregarded from the rate.[3]

---

[2] CRS Report RL32748, *The Temporary Assistance for Needy Families (TANF) Block Grant: A Primer on TANF Financing and Federal Requirements*, by Gene Falk.

[3] For details on the computation of the participation rate, see CRS Report RL32748, *The Temporary Assistance for Needy Families (TANF) Block Grant: A Primer on TANF Financing and Federal Requirements*, by Gene Falk.

Rules for Being "Engaged in Work"

Work-eligible individuals must participate in specific activities during a month to be considered "engaged in work" and have the activities count toward the work participation standard. Most welfare-to-work activities are on the list of activities that count toward the participation standards, including educational and rehabilitative activities. However, there are limits on the ability of states to count participation in pre-employment activities such as education, rehabilitative activities, and job search toward the work standards. For example, teen parents (under the age of 20) may be deemed "engaged in work" through completing high school or obtaining a General Educational Development (GED) diploma. However, for parents age 20 and older, participation in a GED program counts only if the recipient also participates in activities more closely related to work for at least 20 hours per week. Vocational educational training may be counted only for 12 months in a recipient's lifetime. The combination of job search and rehabilitative activities (e.g., rehabilitation from a disability, substance abuse treatment) is limited to a maximum of 12 weeks in a fiscal year.

Work-eligible individuals must also participate in activities for a minimum number of hours per week in a month to be considered "engaged in work." In general, single parents with a pre-school aged child (under the age of six) must participate for at least 20 hours per week in a month; other single parents must participate at least 30 hours per week in a month. Two-parent families face higher hours standards.

Rules for Being "Engaged in Work" and Work Requirements that Apply to Individual Recipients

The work participation standards described above apply to states, not individual recipients. Work requirements applicable to individuals, and the financial sanctions on families with individuals who fail to comply with them, are determined by the states. States may engage recipients in activities that do not count toward the participation standards, require fewer hours than the federal standard, and exempt categories of recipients from work or participation in activities altogether. States that allow participation in activities that cannot be counted (e.g., job search or education in excess of their time limits) do not receive credit for that participation. Depending on the circumstances in the state, lack of credit for certain types of participation or exemptions from requirements might put the state at risk of failing the work standard. Thus, though the work participation standard's counting rules do not apply directly to individual recipients, they may influence how a state designs its welfare-to-work program.

The Caseload Reduction and "Excess MOE" Credits

As discussed above, few jurisdictions have faced the full TANF 50% or 90% work participation standards. This is because of a provision in TANF law known as the caseload reduction credit.

The caseload reduction credit reduces a state's 50% and 90% standards by one percentage point for each percent reduction in its caseload since FY2005. Before FY2007, caseload reduction was measured from FY1995. The Deficit Reduction Act of 2005 (P.L. 109-171) made the change in the credit, measuring caseload reduction from FY2005.

Additionally, under HHS regulations promulgated in 1999, states also may receive credits for spending in excess of what they are required to spend under the MOE requirement.[4] States may consider families assisted by excess MOE as "caseload reduction," and hence receive extra caseload reduction credits for such families.

The American Recovery and Reinvestment Act of 2009 (ARRA, P.L. 111-5) allowed states that experienced caseload increases during the recent recession to freeze their caseload reduction credits at pre-recession levels. This freeze applied only to reductions in work participation standards through FY2011. Additionally, HHS also issued regulations to standardize the calculation of the excess MOE credit.[5] This regulation also might affect future caseload reduction credits.

Trends in "Effective" Work Standards

Since FY2002, the states and territories have faced a statutory work participation standard of 50% for all families.[6] However, in all years but one (FY2007) from FY2002 to FY2009, caseload reduction and/or excess MOE permitted a majority of jurisdictions to face an effective (after-credit) work participation standard of less than 25%. (FY2009 is the latest work participation data available as of July 23, 2012.)

Table 1 shows the number of jurisdictions with effective participation standards of 0%; from 1% to 9.9%; from 10% to 24.9%; from 25% to 49.9%; and 50%. A state-by-state breakdown of TANF effective standards is shown in **Table A-1**. In FY2008 and FY2009, 22 jurisdictions faced a 0% work participation standard. In FY2009, only Guam and South Dakota faced the full 50% standard.

---

[4] These regulations are at 45 C.F.R. §261.43.

[5] U.S. Department of Health and Human Services, "Reauthorization of the Temporary Assistance for Needy Families (TANF) Program; Final Rules ," 73 *Federal Register* 67721-6828, February 5, 2008.

[6] Tribes, tribal organizations, and tribal consortia are authorized to receive and administer their own Tribal Family Assistance Grant for the support of activities that meet the same purposes as state TANF programs. However, tribes are not subject to all of the same work requirements that states are. Though there are hourly minimums and annual targeted participation rates that they must meet, each of these requirements is set by the tribe, in cooperation with the Department of Health and Human Services. At the recipient level, Tribal TANF work activities are not subject to the same restrictions on vocational training as are placed on State TANF programs. Further, tribes may define their own individual work activities that count for the purposes of calculating their work participation rate, so recipients may have a different range of activities that may count toward their own hourly requirements.

Table 1. Effective TANF Work Participation Standards for All Families:
FY2002-FY2009

(number of jurisdictions by category of effective work participation standards)

Effective (After Caseload Reduction and Excess MOE Credit) Participation Standards	2002	2003	2004	2005	2006	2007	2008	2009
Zero	21	20	18	17	19	4	22	22
0%-9.9%	21	15	17	16	14	5	0	1
10%-24.9%	9	15	13	16	15	11	13	16
25%-49.9%	2	3	5	4	5	32	16	13
50%	1	1	1	1	1	2	3	2

Source: Congressional Research Service (CRS) tabulations of data from the U.S. Department of Health and Human Services (HHS).

Note: The 54 jurisdictions operating TANF programs are the 50 states, the District of Columbia, Puerto Rico, Guam, and the Virgin Islands.

Before FY2006, most of the reduction of the work participation standard came from caseload reduction. Nationally, caseloads declined by 57% from FY1995 through FY2005. Caseload reduction credits were much reduced in FY2007, when credits were based on caseload change only from FY2005 to FY2006. In that year, only four jurisdictions faced a zero participation standard. However, beginning in FY2008 states began to rely on the "excess MOE" portion of the caseload reduction credit, and effective standards were substantially reduced again. The Government Accountability Office (GAO) found that in FY2009, 16 states would not have met their TANF work participation standards had they not claimed excess MOE credits.[7]

As discussed above, the ARRA caseload reduction credit freeze expires beginning with the FY2012 work participation standards. HHS rules standardizing the calculation of the excess MOE portion of that credit could also affect the size of future credits and effective rates.

Trends in Work Participation Rates

Figure 1 shows the national average work participation rate based on the federal rules for FY2002 through FY2009. This participation rate measures the extent to which families are considered "engaged in work" under the TANF statute. The rate shown on the figure excludes the effect of "grandfathered" pre-1996 welfare law waivers. These waivers are discussed below. The figure shows that the participation rate has fluctuated around 30% since FY2002, remaining well below 50% for the entire period. However, most states met their participation standards with rates below 50% because of caseload reduction and excess MOE credits.

---

[7] U.S. Government Accountability Office, *Temporary Assistance for Needy Families. State Maintenance of Effort and Trends. Testimony Before the Subcommittee on Human Resources, Committee On Ways and Means, House of Representatives*, GAO-12-713T, May 17, 2012, p. 13.

Figure 1. National Average TANF Work Participation Rate: FY2002-FY2009

(based on federal rules; excludes "grandfathered" pre-1996 welfare waivers for FY2002-FY2007)

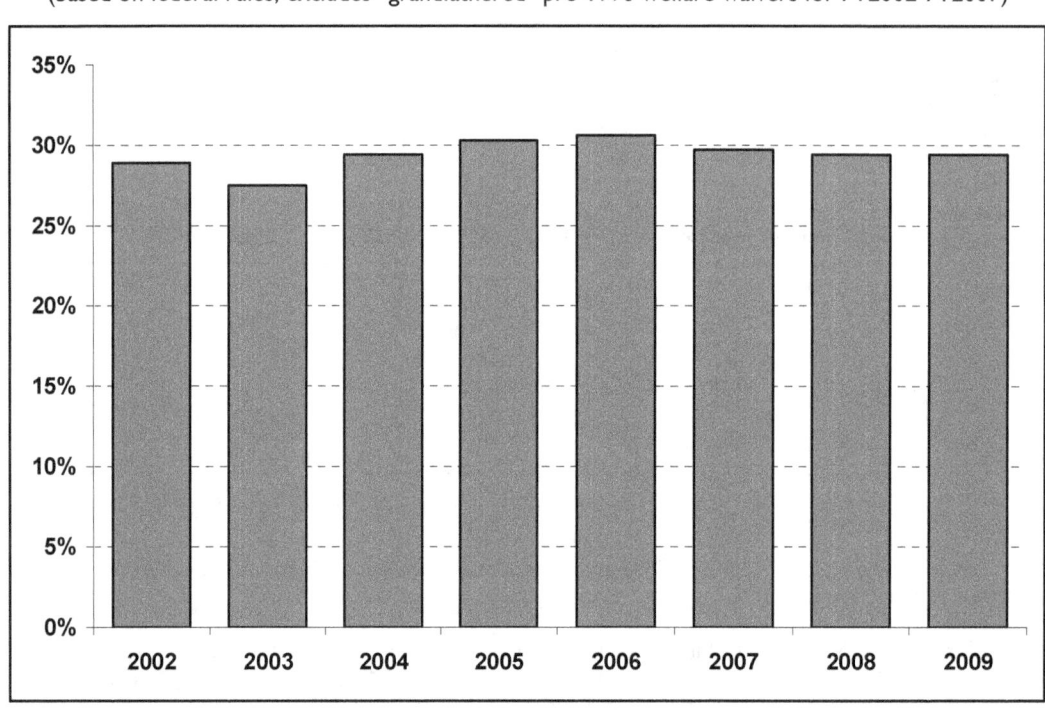

Source: Congressional Research Service (CRS), based on data from the U.S. Department of Health and Human Services (HHS).

Two-Parent Families

Historically, most families receiving cash assistance have been single-parent families, usually headed by a single mother. However, some two-parent families receive assistance. Under TANF's work participation standards, these families are subject to a higher standard: 90% of these families must be engaged in work, though the two-parent standard can also be reduced for caseload reduction. Additionally, more hours of participation are required of two-parent families. The work-eligible adults in two-parent families must participate in activities for at least 35 hours per week in a month; if the family receives federally funded child care, at least 55 hours per week in a month are required. (The hours requirement applies to the total hours of engagement by both parents.)

Many states have avoided the need to meet the two-parent family standard. Before FY2007, many states aided two-parent families in "separate state programs." Separate state programs are state programs with expenditures counted toward the TANF MOE but not considered TANF programs. Before FY2007, cash assistance families in separate state programs were not included in the work participation rate and thus not subject to TANF's work participation standards. The Deficit Reduction Act of 2005 (P.L. 109-171) brought families in separate state programs into the calculation of TANF participation rates, thus subjecting them to the standards effective in FY2007. However, many states then moved these families to "solely state funded programs," with expenditures that are not countable toward TANF's MOE and thus totally outside of TANF's rules including work participation. In FY2009, 28 jurisdictions had two-parent families included in their TANF or MOE caseloads.

Secretary's Flexibility in Assessing Penalties for Failure to Meet Work Standards

The TANF statute gives the Secretary of HHS flexibility in assessing the financial penalty (reduction in the block grant) for failure to meet work participation standards. The Secretary may reduce the penalty based on the degree of noncompliance, waive the penalty if a state demonstrates "good cause," and enter into corrective compliance plans with states and subsequently forgive them if they come into compliance with the work standards.

Legislative Status of TANF

The five-year extension of TANF funding enacted in the Deficit Reduction Act of 2005 (P.L. 109-171) expired at the end of FY2010. President Obama's Administration has not made a legislative proposal to reauthorize TANF. However, in its FY2013 budget submission, the Administration did set forth some general principles for TANF reauthorization:

> When Congress takes up reauthorization, we want to work with lawmakers to strengthen the program's effectiveness in accomplishing its goals. This should include using performance indicators to drive program improvement and ensuring that states have the flexibility to engage recipients in the most effective activities to promote success in the workforce – including families with serious barriers to employment. We also want to work with Congress to revise the Contingency Fund to make it more effective during economic downturns.[8]

Since the end of FY2010, Congress has enacted several short-term extensions of TANF. The latest, included in the legislation that extended the payroll tax reduction and unemployment benefits (P.L. 112-96), expires on September 30, 2012. That is, Congress must act if it is to continue TANF beyond the end of the current fiscal year.

The Obama Administration's Waiver Initiative

HHS has indicated a willingness to grant certain waivers of the federal TANF work participation standards. It says these waivers would be granted under Section 1115 of the Social Security Act.[9] This initiative was announced on July 12, 2012. HHS said in its announcement that this initiative is a response to President Obama's February 28, 2011, Presidential memorandum that asked agencies to work with state, local, and tribal grantees of federal funds to identify barriers "that

---

[8] U.S. Department of Health and Human Services, *FY2013 Budget in Brief*, February 2012, p. 5.

[9] Section 1115 of the Social Security Act permits the Secretary of HHS to waive TANF state plan requirements specified in Section 402 of the Social Security Act to conduct an "experimental, pilot, or demonstration project which, in the judgment of the Secretary, is likely to assist in promoting the objectives" of the federal law. The TANF state plan is a document states must submit as a condition of receiving its block grant. The Secretary must find that a state plan is complete in order for block grant funds to be awarded to a state. Part of the state plan is an outline of the family assistance program the state intends to operate, which includes a requirement that it ensure "that parents and caretakers receiving assistance under the program engage in work activities" in accordance with the TANF work participation standards in Section 407 of the Social Security Act.

currently prevent states, localities, and tribes from efficiently using tax dollars to achieve the best results for their constituents."[10]

The waiver programs would allow states that undertake alternative welfare-to-work strategies to substitute other performance measures (e.g., outcome measures) for the TANF statutory work participation standards. Waiver programs would also have to be formally evaluated. Waivers could be granted for state-wide initiatives, or demonstrations and pilots conducted in a portion of the state. These initiatives could also be either for a state's entire caseload, or a specific population within its caseload (e.g., individuals with disabilities). HHS envisions the typical waiver as having a five-year duration. The HHS announcement also says states may receive waivers of the existing procedures to verify participation put into place through the Deficit Reduction Act of 2005.

Goals of the Waiver

HHS says a goal of its waiver initiative is to allow states to operate experimental, pilot, or demonstration projects to test "alternative and innovative strategies, policies, and procedures that are designed to improve employment outcomes for needy families." The department says it is "encouraging states to consider new, more effective ways to meet the goals of TANF, particularly helping parents successfully prepare for, find, and retain employment." In its announcement, HHS noted that waivers of TANF work participation standards could address the following goals: improving coordination with other programs, such as programs operated under the Workforce Investment Act (WIA); testing multiyear career pathways models that combine work and learning; strengthening strategies for individuals with disabilities; testing the effectiveness of subsidized employment programs; and testing the effectiveness of extending the period of time allowed for participation in pre-employment activities such as vocational educational training and job search and readiness.

The department says that another goal of the waiver initiative is to develop a new body of research evidence that could improve state programs' abilities to achieve TANF's goals.

Application and Approval Process

In order for TANF work standards to be waived, states would have to apply for a waiver and have that waiver approved by HHS and OMB. HHS has specified some elements that will be required of waiver requests: they must include a set of performance measures; an evaluation plan; the proposed duration of the waiver; and a budget that includes the cost of evaluation.

Ongoing Performance Monitoring and Evaluation

HHS has said that states will be required to track ongoing performance and outcomes during the period of the demonstration projects. States applying for waivers must set interim performance targets. States that fail to meet interim targets would be required to develop improvement plans. HHS asserts that repeated failure to meet performance targets will lead to an end of the waiver

---

[10] This memorandum can be found at http://www.whitehouse.gov/the-press-office/2011/02/28/presidential-memorandum-administrative-flexibility.

demonstration. In a correspondence to Members of Congress, HHS Secretary Kathleen Sebelius stated that states would be required to increase the number of people moving from welfare-to-work by at least 20%.[11]

HHS says that its "preferred" approach to evaluating programs is a random assignment experiment.[12] However, HHS notes it will consider alternative methods for evaluating the waiver demonstration program.

What Will Not be Waived

HHS has said that it will not waive requirements that would reduce access to assistance or employment. Moreover, a number of TANF provisions are outside the scope of the requirements to be waived (e.g., TANF time limits and child support enforcement requirements).

Implications for Welfare-to-Work Programs

As discussed above, TANF work participation standards do not apply directly to individuals, though they may influence the design of a state's welfare-to-work strategy. Allowing states alternative ways of assessing state welfare-to-work efforts might also influence a state's strategy. If performance is tracked using an outcome measure (e.g., rate of entry into employment of TANF recipients), states would no longer risk failing a standard solely by having recipients engaged in activities that do not count toward a participation rate. Such additional participation might include allowing recipients to engage in pre-employment activities (job search, rehabilitative activities, education) beyond the TANF work standard's limits and restrictions. However, if that participation is ineffective in helping the state achieve a good score on the new outcome measure, the state would risk failing the new performance standards.

Pre-1996 Welfare Waivers

Waivers issued under the Obama Administration's initiative would be the first waivers to test alternative welfare-to-work approaches in over 15 years. The Public Welfare Amendments of 1962 (P.L. 87-543) established waiver authority within Section 1115 of the Social Security Act for public assistance programs, including the Aid to Families with Dependent Children (AFDC) program that preceded TANF in helping fund cash assistance for needy families with children.

Though waivers under Section 1115 were allowed as early as 1962, they were not sought with much frequency until the late 1980s. Until that point, waivers were primarily related to program administration and service delivery.[13] Between 1987 and 1989, during the Reagan Administration,

---

[11] Letter from Kathleen Sebelius, Secretary of HHS, to Dave Camp, Chairman, House Committee on Ways and Means, (July 18, 2012) available at http://www.washingtonpost.com/blogs/ezra-klein/files/2012/07/Chairman-Camp-TANF-7-18-.pdf A similar letter was sent to Senator Orrin G. Hatch, Ranking Member of the Senate Finance Committee, available at http://www.washingtonpost.com/blogs/ezra-klein/files/2012/07/Sen-Hatch-TANF-7-18-.pdf

[12] These types of studies assign potential participations to two or more groups: one, a control group that is subject to existing policies (e.g., no change in the program); the others would be an experimental group or groups that are subject to new policies. The difference in outcomes between the experimental group(s) and the control group measures the impact of the policy change.

[13] See Shelly Arsneault, *Welfare Policy Innovation and Diffusion: Section 1115 Waivers and the Federal System*, State (continued...)

---

15 waiver applications for welfare reform were approved for 14 states; during the Administration of George H.W. Bush, another 15 applications from 12 states were approved. Until the enactment of the 1996 welfare law, the Clinton Administration continued to approve waivers of AFDC law. Between January 1993 and August 1996, a total of 83 waiver applications from 43 states and the District of Columbia were approved.

In order to receive and implement a waiver, a state was required to conduct a structured evaluation of its proposed program, which featured an "impact analysis" that assessed the success of the program in meeting its goals. "Impacts" included employment and earnings as well as indicators of child well-being, like school attendance and health. Evaluations often combined both qualitative and quantitative methods, utilizing sources such as surveys, program data, and in-depth interviews.[14] The waiver process sometimes also required approval by the state legislature of proposed program changes, usually before the proposal was submitted to HHS.[15]

Waivers ranged in scope from small demonstrations that were carried out in a select number of counties to greater statewide changes in the state's AFDC program. In many cases, a state's AFDC waiver program became the basis for its TANF program following the enactment of federal welfare reform in 1996. They tested program features such as requiring mothers of young children to participate in work or activities, stronger sanctions for failure to comply with participation requirements, the impact of providing earnings supplements to families, and time limits.

Grandfathering of Pre-1996 Welfare Waivers Under TANF

The 1996 welfare reform law allowed states to delay implementation of certain TANF provisions to the extent that they were inconsistent with requirements of the state's approved waiver demonstration project (if the state chose to continue its waiver). States that continued their work-related waivers were permitted to have their programs assessed based on the rules of their waivers, rather than those of the federal work participation standard.[16] In general, states that operated under waivers still had to achieve the numerical participation standards required under the new law.[17] However, they were able to count certain participation that otherwise would not meet the federal definition of "engaged in work."[18] This included activities not countable toward

---

(...continued)

and Local Government Review, Vol. 32, No. 1 (Winter 2000), pp. 49-60. (Hereinafter cited as Shelly Arsneault, 2000).

[14] See Carol Harvey, Michael J. Camasso, and Radha Jagannathan, *Evaluating Welfare Reform Waivers Under Section 1115*, Journal of Economic Perspectives, Volume 14, Number 4, Fall 2000, pp. 165-188.

[15] See Shelly Arsneault, 2000.

[16] As described in the preamble to the TANF Final Rule, a "work-related waiver" included both the explicitly granted technical waiver and the cluster of related work policies that were in effect under prior law and continued as part of the state's demonstration. These could include provisions regarding allowable activities, hours, or exemptions. See U.S. Department of Health and Human Services, Administration for Children and Families, "Temporary Assistance for Needy Families Program (TANF); Final Rule," 64 *Federal Register* 17731-17739, April 12, 1999.

[17] Vermont claimed that its waiver exempted all families from the participation rate calculation. HHS did not publish a participation rate for Vermont for FY2000 or FY2001.

[18] See 6th Annual Report to Congress, November 2004. Accessible at http://www.acf.hhs.gov/programs/ofa/data-reports/annualreport6/ar6index.htm.

the participation standard, such as extended job search and education. It also included families participating for fewer hours than required under that federal definition. Further, states were also permitted to exclude from the participation rate calculation families that were exempted from the welfare-to-work program under their waiver.[19]

TANF regulations required states to certify by October 1, 1999, whether or not they intended to continue their waiver policies until the scheduled expiration of the waiver. A total of 20 states continued their waiver policies with respect to work requirements.[20] **Figure 2** shows the number of states operating under these "grandfathered" waivers in FY2000 through FY2007. The number gradually declined from FY2000 through FY2007 as these waivers expired. **Table A-4** describes the specific waiver inconsistencies claimed by each state under the grandfathered waiver.

Figure 2. Number of States Operating TANF Under "Grandfathered" Pre-1996 Welfare Reform Waivers : FY2000-FY2007.

(includes states operating waivers for part of the fiscal year)

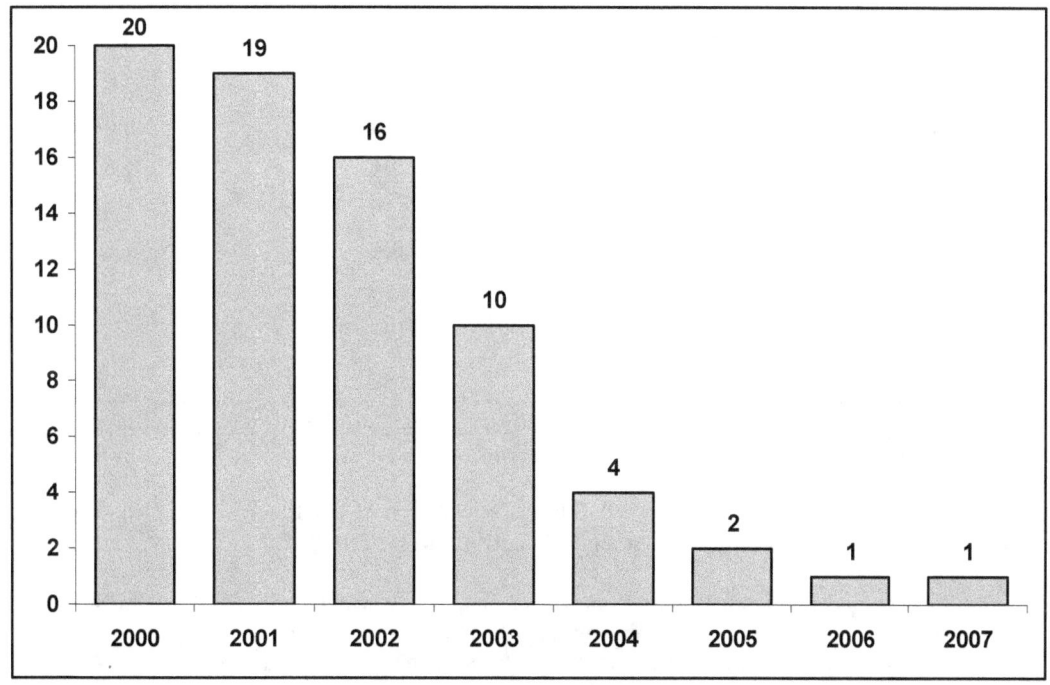

Source: Congressional Research Service (CRS), based on data from the U.S. Department of Health and Human Services (HHS).

As described above, states with waivers had their welfare-to-work programs assessed using the rules of the waiver rather than the rules of the federal work participation standard. For FY2000 through FY2006, HHS calculated two sets of work participation rates: the official rate (using the

---

[19] See *Federal Register*, April 12, 1999 (Volume 64, Number 69), p. 17734.

[20] For a full list of states claiming work requirement waiver inconsistencies, see pp. 201-203 of the 3rd Annual Report to Congress, available at http://www.acf.hhs.gov/programs/ofa/data-reports/annual3/annual3.pdf. For a full list of states claiming time limit waiver inconsistencies, see pp. 233-234 of the same report.

waiver rules for those states with grandfathered waivers) and a rate based on the federal rules for the work standard (shown on **Figure 1**).

Table 2 shows the effect "grandfathered" waivers had on the national average TANF work participation rate. In FY2001 and FY2002, waivers added 4.5 percentage points to the national average participation rate. In other words, a greater proportion of TANF families was counted as engaged in work under the waivers than under the statutory TANF work participation standards. This declined in subsequent years, as the number of states operating their programs under these waivers declined. **Table A-5** and **Table A-6** show the work participation rates with and without the effect of the "grandfathered" waivers for the 20 states that continued them under TANF.

Table 2. National Average TANF Work Participation Rate for FY2000 through FY2009: With and Without the Effect of "Grandfathered" Waivers

Year	With Waivers	Without Waivers	Difference
2000	34.0%	29.7%	4.3
2001	34.4%	29.9%	4.5
2002	33.4%	28.9%	4.5
2003	31.3%	27.5%	3.8
2004	32.2%	29.4%	2.8
2005	33.0%	30.3%	2.7
2006	32.5%	30.6%	1.9
2007		29.7%	
2008		29.4%	
2009		29.4%	

Source: Congressional Research Service (CRS), based on data from the U.S. Department of Health and Human Services (HHS).

In its 2002 TANF reauthorization proposal, the Administration of George W. Bush proposed to immediately end the "grandfathered waivers." According to the Administration's proposal:

> Flexibility under current law allows states to accomplish all the purposes of TANF without waivers. Furthermore, the requirements of TANF no longer represent an experiment. Abolishing the remaining waivers will put all states on an equal footing.[21]

The Administration's proposal was not adopted. The last of the waivers (Tennessee's) expired in 2007.

The "Superwaiver" Proposal

Though the Bush Administration's 2002 TANF reauthorization proposal sought to end the "grandfathered waivers," it concurrently proposed new waiver authority that would have applied

---

[21] See *Working Toward Independence: Maximize Self Sufficiency Through Work and Additional Constructive Activities,* February 2002, http://georgewbush-whitehouse.archives.gov/news/releases/2002/02/welfare-book-04.html.

to TANF. The "superwaiver" proposal would have allowed states to seek "new waivers for integrating funding and program rules across a broad range of public assistance and workforce development programs."[22] States that received waivers would have been required to develop integrated performance objectives and outcomes, which could have altered reporting and performance requirements in affected programs. An evaluation of the demonstration would have been required.

The superwaiver proposal passed the House three times: in 2002, 2003, and 2005.[23] The legislation would have had the effect of allowing TANF work participation standards to be waived. A scaled back version of the superwaiver was also included in bills reported by the Senate Finance Committee in 2003 and 2005.[24]

Legislation

Legislation has been introduced to halt the Obama Administration's current waiver initiative. H.R. 6140 (Representative Camp) and S. 3397 (Senator Hatch) would prohibit HHS from granting a waiver of the work participation standards. Additionally, it would rescind any waiver issued before the bill's enactment. As introduced, the bills' findings sections question the secretary's legal authority to grant waivers of TANF work requirements.

In a decision released on September 4, 2012, the Government Accountability Office (GAO) determined that the waiver initiative constitutes a "rule," subject to the Congressional Review Act (CRA).[25] The CRA sets procedures for Congress to consider a resolution of disapproval of new rules.[26] Under the CRA, if a "resolution of disapproval" is passed by Congress and signed by the President (or the President's veto is overridden), the waiver initiative could not take effect. On September 20, 2012, the House passed such a "resolution of disapproval" (H.J.Res. 118) of the waiver initiative. A "resolution of disapproval" of the waiver initiative (S.J.Res. 50) has also been introduced in the Senate by Senator Hatch.

---

[22] For a discussion of the superwaiver, CRS Report RS21219, *"Superwaiver" Proposals in the Welfare Reform Debate*, by Karen Spar.

[23] The bills that passed the House are H.R. 4737 (107th Congress), passed the House on May 16, 2002; H.R. 4 (108th Congress), passed the House on February 13, 2003; and S. 1932 (109th Congress), passed the House on November 18, 2005.

[24] The bills approved by the Senate Finance Committee are H.R. 4 (108th Congress), as amended, reported on October 3, 2003; and S. 667 (109th Congress), ordered reported on March 9, 2005.

[25] See U.S. Government Accountability Office, Temporary Assistance For Needy Families: Information Memorandum Constitutes Rule for the Purposes of the Congressional Review Act, B-3237772, September 4, 2012, http://www.gao.gov/assets/650/647778.pdf.

[26] A discussion of the Congressional Review Act can be found in CRS Report RL32240, *The Federal Rulemaking Process: An Overview*, by Maeve P. Carey.

Appendix.

Table A-1. Effective TANF Work Participation Standards by State: FY2002-FY2009

(effective standards are after caseload reduction credits, including excess MOE credits)

State	2002	2003	2004	2005	2006	2007	2008	2009
Alabama	0.0%	0.0%	0.0%	0.0%	0.0%	0.0%	0.0%	0.0%
Alaska	8.7	11.1	6.9	4.8	6.8	32.5	25.8	21.4
Arizona	4.8	13.1	19.6	24.0	11.6	7.3	0.0	0.0
Arkansas	0.0	3.3	4.3	3.9	2.7	0.0	0.0	0.0
California	6.7	5.8	3.9	4.5	5.1	32.3	29.0	29.0
Colorado	0.0	0.0	0.0	0.0	0.0	15.1	0.0	0.0
Connecticut	21.0	20.3	20.2	23.4	23.4	12.7	0.0	0.0
Delaware	6.7	10.2	12.5	17.6	18.2	26.1	0.0	0.0
District of Columbia	11.2	11.5	13.3	15.3	14.4	32.5	31.9	31.9
Florida	0.0	0.0	0.0	0.0	0.0	2.4	0.0	0.0
Georgia	0.0	0.0	4.3	5.9	0.0	26.0	13.8	12.3
Hawaii	26.6	20.0	16.4	12.1	0.0	20.8	0.0	0.0
Idaho	15.9	20.0	34.5	27.9	28.5	43.1	38.1	30.6
Illinois	0.0	0.0	0.0	0.0	0.0	44.7	0.0	0.0
Indiana	15.4	28.9	35.4	33.4	27.1	46.5	11.3	11.3
Iowa	6.4	7.3	8.8	11.0	17.3	25.7	24.0	24.0
Kansas	38.4	41.7	37.6	38.8	38.8	11.5	0.0	0.0
Kentucky	2.9	4.5	6.2	10.1	11.9	41.7	36.6	31.9
Louisiana	0.0	0.0	0.0	0.0	0.0	24.0	17.4	15.2
Maine	1.9	2.5	0.0	1.1	2.9	31.4	47.5	47.5
Maryland	6.2	6.5	6.6	6.5	5.2	34.1	31.7	31.7
Massachusetts	0.8	4.9	6.3	8.4	8.5	14.3	0.0	0.0
Michigan	0.0	0.0	0.0	0.0	0.0	30.5	50.0	27.8
Minnesota	12.9	14.8	18.6	18.8	14.9	44.6	0.0	0.0
Mississippi	12.5	12.6	17.1	5.4	4.1	33.5	22.2	20.2
Missouri	5.7	5.0	3.7	4.5	2.8	7.4	14.9	14.9
Montana	0.0	2.0	10.8	13.2	16.3	26.1	26.0	25.8
Nebraska	17.6	24.2	28.7	28.6	31.1	23.0	0.0	0.0
Nevada	4.1	26.2	31.8	10.3	10.7	38.6	34.5	31.2
New Hampshire	2.4	6.1	7.8	7.4	8.4	9.5	0.0	0.0
New Jersey	0.0	0.0	0.0	0.0	0.0	0.0	0.0	0.0

State	2002	2003	2004	2005	2006	2007	2008	2009
New Mexico	8.3	8.4	8.2	12.0	13.2	46.2	15.2	15.2
New York	0.0	0.0	0.0	0.0	0.0	13.8	11.5	11.5
North Carolina	0.0	0.0	0.0	0.0	0.0	22.1	0.0	0.0
North Dakota	7.5	12.0	14.7	8.8	4.8	44.0	23.1	20.8
Ohio	0.0	0.0	9.7	15.7	19.1	46.2	42.0	42.0
Oklahoma	2.9	0.0	0.0	0.0	0.0	34.6	28.8	20.6
Oregon	0.0	0.0	0.0	0.0	0.3	45.1	45.4	45.4
Pennsylvania	0.0	0.0	0.0	0.0	0.0	42.0	19.7	15.8
Puerto Rico	0.0	3.1	0.0	0.0	0.0	44.6	40.3	23.5
Rhode Island	22.9	19.2	15.4	13.1	10.7	8.0	0.0	0.0
South Carolina	0.7	2.4	3.0	3.0	3.3	29.0	0.0	0.0
South Dakota	9.3	12.4	11.7	10.9	13.7	50.0	50.0	50.0
Tennessee	7.8	11.6	11.6	19.6	19.1	35.5	0.0	0.0
Texas	0.0	0.0	0.9	0.0	0.0	31.2	19.9	10.8
Utah	11.7	17.0	24.6	17.8	27.3	32.6	10.1	5.4
Vermont	8.8	7.1	5.7	5.5	2.4	23.0	11.1	11.1
Virginia	0.0	0.0	0.0	0.1	0.8	36.0	38.5	37.8
Washington	7.0	8.2	8.8	6.9	10.7	11.1	0.0	0.0
West Virginia	0.0	0.0	0.0	0.0	0.0	39.2	26.3	17.4
Wisconsin	0.0	0.0	0.4	1.3	0.0	30.9	0.0	0.0
Wyoming	0.0	0.0	0.0	0.0	0.0	47.3	35.3	34.2
Guam	50.0	50.0	50.0	50.0	50.0	50.0	50.0	50.0
Virgin Islands	6.5	0.0	0.0	0.0	0.0	0.0	0.0	0.0

Number of States with Effective (After-Credit) TANF Work Participation Standards Equal to:

Zero	21	20	18	17	19	4	22	22
0%-9.9%	21	15	17	16	14	5	0	1
10%-24.9%	9	15	13	16	15	11	13	16
25%-49.9%	2	3	5	4	5	32	16	13
50%	1	1	1	1	1	2	3	2

Source: Congressional Research Service (CRS), based on data from the U.S. Department of Health and Human Services (HHS).

Table A-2. TANF Work Participation Rates by State: Official Rates
(Including Grandfathered Waivers): FY2002-FY2009

	2002	2003	2004	2005	2006	2007	2008	2009
Alabama	37.3%	37.1%	37.9%	38.6%	41.6%	34.0%	37.4%	32.4%
Alaska	39.6	41.1	43.6	45.7	45.6	46.8	42.8	37.2
Arizona	25.9	13.4	25.5	30.3	29.6	30.0	27.8	27.1
Arkansas	21.4	22.4	27.3	28.3	27.9	35.3	38.8	37.1
California	27.3	24.0	23.1	25.9	22.2	22.3	25.1	26.8
Colorado	35.9	32.5	34.7	25.8	30.0	27.3	32.3	37.8
Connecticut	26.6	30.6	24.3	33.8	30.8	28.8	25.3	34.4
Delaware	25.8	18.2	22.1	22.6	25.3	32.7	48.8	37.5
District of Columbia	16.4	23.1	18.2	23.5	17.1	35.0	49.6	23.5
Florida	30.4	33.1	40.4	38.0	41.0	64.2	42.4	46.1
Georgia	8.2	10.9	24.8	57.2	64.9	54.2	59.0	57.1
Hawaii	58.8	65.8	70.5	35.5	37.3	28.7	34.4	40.3
Idaho	40.7	43.7	41.0	39.9	44.2	53.0	59.5	52.0
Illinois	58.4	57.8	46.1	43.0	53.0	55.5	42.6	49.3
Indiana	62.6	40.3	36.3	30.9	26.7	27.5	29.4	17.5
Iowa	51.2	45.1	50.0	47.8	39.0	40.2	41.1	35.4
Kansas	84.8	87.9	88.0	86.7	77.2	12.8	19.6	23.9
Kentucky	32.4	32.8	38.1	39.7	44.6	38.2	38.0	37.3
Louisiana	38.7	34.6	35.4	34.6	38.4	42.2	40.0	34.4
Maine	44.5	27.7	32.1	28.3	26.6	21.9	11.4	16.8
Maryland	8.3	9.1	16.0	20.5	44.5	46.7	36.9	44.0
Massachusetts	60.9	61.0	60.0	59.9	13.6	17.0	44.7	47.5
Michigan	28.9	25.3	24.5	22.0	21.6	28.0	33.6	27.9
Minnesota	40.4	25.0	26.8	28.9	30.3	28.1	29.9	29.8
Mississippi	18.5	17.2	21.0	22.6	35.5	61.9	63.2	67.5
Missouri	25.4	28.0	19.5	20.0	18.7	14.0	14.2	13.2
Montana	84.2	85.9	92.7	83.1	79.2	46.4	44.2	44.2
Nebraska	28.1	33.4	34.5	31.8	32.0	23.0	51.2	50.3
Nevada	21.6	22.3	34.5	42.3	47.8	34.0	42.1	39.4
New Hampshire	41.8	28.2	30.2	24.6	24.1	42.0	47.4	46.5
New Jersey	36.4	35.0	34.6	29.0	29.2	33.0	18.9	20.1
New Mexico	42.7	42.0	46.2	41.6	42.3	36.4	37.5	43.1
New York	38.5	37.1	37.8	35.2	37.8	38.0	37.3	33.4

	2002	2003	2004	2005	2006	2007	2008	2009
North Carolina	27.4	25.3	31.4	27.5	32.4	32.4	24.5	32.3
North Dakota	30.4	27.0	25.3	31.4	51.9	58.7	50.2	61.0
Ohio	56.3	62.3	65.2	58.3	54.9	23.7	24.5	23.3
Oklahoma	26.7	29.2	33.2	34.0	32.9	38.1	29.2	23.0
Oregon	61.1	60.0	32.1	14.9	15.2	14.7	24.1	9.5
Pennsylvania	10.4	9.9	7.1	15.2	26.1	48.9	38.6	45.8
Puerto Rico	5.6	6.1	7.5	13.1	13.1	8.2	11.6	8.7
Rhode Island	24.6	24.3	23.7	24.2	24.9	26.8	17.5	13.8
South Carolina	52.4	54.3	53.7	54.3	49.5	53.3	51.7	45.1
South Dakota	42.5	46.1	54.8	57.5	57.9	53.5	62.2	59.4
Tennessee	41.2	42.7	50.6	52.1	57.2	45.9	25.2	25.5
Texas	30.8	28.1	34.2	38.9	42.0	34.6	29.3	37.0
Utah	27.9	28.1	26.2	30.3	42.5	49.8	37.6	32.6
Vermont	21.4	24.3	24.9	22.4	22.2	22.4	23.2	29.0
Virginia	42.9	44.6	50.1	46.3	53.9	43.5	45.4	44.3
Washington	49.8	46.2	35.4	38.6	36.1	25.4	18.3	23.0
West Virginia	19.2	14.2	11.7	16.3	26.2	15.4	.17.6	19.6
Wisconsin	69.4	67.2	61.3	44.3	36.2	36.7	37.1	39.9
Wyoming	82.9	83.0	77.8	82.1	77.2	65.4	50.5	61.3
Guam	0.0	0.0	0.0	0.0	0.0	2.5	0.0	0.0
Virgin Islands	17.7	5.0	10.6	16.9	14.5	17.1	15.5	7.1

Number of States with Participation Rates Equal to:

0% - 9.9%	4	5	3	1	1	2	1	4
10%-24.9%	9	11	13	14	11	11	13	11
25%-34%	14	16	15	15	14	15	11	12
35%-49.9%	15	12	11	15	18	17	21	20
50% or more	12	10	12	9	10	9	8	7

Source: Congressional Research Service (CRS), based on data from the U.S. Department of Health and Human Services (HHS).

Table A-3. TANF Work Participation Rates Excluding the Effect of "Grandfathered Waivers" by State: FY2002-FY2009

	2002	2003	2004	2005	2006	2007	2008	2009
Alabama	37.3%	37.1%	37.9%	38.6%	41.6%	34.0%	37.4%	32.4%
Alaska	39.6	41.1	43.6	45.7	45.6	46.8	42.8	37.2
Arizona	25.9	13.4	25.5	30.3	29.6	30.0	27.8	27.1
Arkansas	21.4	22.4	27.3	28.3	27.9	35.3	38.8	37.1
California	27.3	24.0	23.1	25.9	22.2	22.3	25.1	26.8
Colorado	35.9	32.5	34.7	25.8	30.0	27.3	32.3	37.8
Connecticut	26.6	30.6	24.3	33.8	30.8	28.8	25.3	34.4
Delaware	11.7	18.2	22.1	22.6	25.3	32.7	48.8	37.5
District of Columbia	16.4	23.1	18.2	23.5	17.1	35.0	49.6	23.5
Florida	30.4	33.1	40.4	38.0	41.0	64.2	42.4	46.1
Georgia	8.2	10.9	24.8	57.2	64.9	54.2	59.0	57.1
Hawaii	32.5	34.6	40.3	35.5	37.3	28.7	34.4	40.3
Idaho	40.7	43.7	41.0	39.9	44.2	53.0	59.5	52.0
Illinois	58.4	57.8	46.1	43.0	53.0	55.5	42.6	49.3
Indiana	45.3	40.3	36.3	30.9	26.7	27.5	29.4	17.5
Iowa	51.2	45.1	50.0	47.8	39.0	40.2	41.1	35.4
Kansas	37.6	32.4	88.0	86.7	77.2	12.8	19.6	23.9
Kentucky	32.4	32.8	38.1	39.7	44.6	38.2	38.0	37.3
Louisiana	38.7	34.6	35.4	34.6	38.4	42.2	40.0	34.4
Maine	44.5	27.7	32.1	28.3	26.6	21.9	11.4	16.8
Maryland	8.3	9.1	16.0	20.5	44.5	46.7	36.9	44.0
Massachusetts	9.2	8.4	10.3	12.6	13.6	17.0	44.7	47.5
Michigan	28.9	25.3	24.5	22.0	21.6	28.0	33.6	27.9
Minnesota	31.2	25.0	26.8	28.9	30.3	28.1	29.9	29.8
Mississippi	18.5	17.2	21.0	22.6	35.5	61.9	63.2	67.5
Missouri	25.4	28.0	19.5	20.0	18.7	14.0	14.2	13.2
Montana	37.9	37.4	86.7	83.1	79.2	46.4	44.2	44.2
Nebraska	22.8	29.4	34.5	31.8	32.0	23.0	51.2	50.3
Nevada	21.6	22.3	34.5	42.3	47.8	34.0	42.1	39.4
New Hampshire	32.6	28.2	30.2	24.6	24.1	42.0	47.4	46.5
New Jersey	36.4	35.0	34.6	29.0	29.2	33.0	18.9	20.1
New Mexico	42.7	42.0	46.2	41.6	42.3	36.4	37.5	43.1
New York	38.5	37.1	37.8	35.2	37.8	38.0	37.3	33.4

	2002	2003	2004	2005	2006	2007	2008	2009
North Carolina	27.4	25.3	31.4	27.5	32.4	32.4	24.5	32.3
North Dakota	30.4	27.0	25.3	31.4	51.9	58.7	50.2	61.0
Ohio	56.1	62.2	65.2	58.3	54.9	23.7	24.5	23.3
Oklahoma	26.7	29.2	33.2	34.0	32.9	38.1	29.2	23.0
Oregon	8.0	14.7	32.1	14.9	15.2	14.7	24.1	9.5
Pennsylvania	10.4	9.9	7.1	15.2	26.1	48.9	38.6	45.8
Puerto Rico	5.6	6.1	7.5	13.1	13.1	8.2	11.6	8.7
Rhode Island	24.6	24.3	23.7	24.2	24.9	26.8	17.5	13.8
South Carolina	30.2	28.6	53.7	54.3	49.5	53.3	51.7	45.1
South Dakota	42.5	46.1	54.8	57.5	57.9	53.5	62.2	59.4
Tennessee	14.3	13.4	13.0	14.3	16.8	45.9	25.2	25.5
Texas	21.1	28.1	34.2	38.9	42.0	34.6	29.3	37.0
Utah	27.9	28.1	26.2	30.3	42.5	49.8	37.6	32.6
Vermont	21.4	24.3	24.9	22.4	22.2	22.4	23.2	29.0
Virginia	22.6	29.9	50.1	46.3	53.9	43.5	45.4	44.3
Washington	49.8	46.2	35.4	38.6	36.1	25.4	18.3	23.0
West Virginia	19.2	14.2	11.7	16.3	26.2	15.4	17.6	19.6
Wisconsin	69.4	67.2	61.3	44.3	36.2	36.7	37.1	39.9
Wyoming	82.9	83.0	77.8	82.1	77.2	65.4	50.5	61.3
Guam	0.0	0.0	0.0	0.0	0.0	2.5	0.0	0.0
Virgin Islands	17.7	5.0	10.6	16.9	14.5	17.1	15.5	7.1

Number of States with Participation Rates Equal to:

	2002	2003	2004	2005	2006	2007	2008	2009
0% - 9.9%	6	6	3	1	1	2	1	4
10%-24.9%	14	13	15	16	12	11	13	11
25%-34%	15	20	15	15	14	15	11	12
35%-49.9%	14	11	12	15	18	17	21	20
50% or more	5	4	9	7	9	9	8	7

Source: Congressional Research Service (CRS), based on data from the U.S. Department of Health and Human Services (HHS).

Table A-4. Grandfathered Pre-1996 Welfare Waivers Under TANF

State	Waiver Expiration Date	Exemptions	Activities/Hours	Other
Arizona	9/30/02	No additional exemptions.	No waiver provision.	Sanctions are for failure (rather than refusal) to participate in required activities.
Connecticut	9/30/01	Exempts individuals who are incapacitated, of advanced age, needed in the home to care for an incapacitated household member, certain pregnant or postpartum women, and an individual otherwise deemed unemployable.	Allows any of the 12 federally approved activities (without priority/secondary distinction) to count toward the work participation rate. Hours required depends on the activity and the individual. Maximum number of required hours per week is 35 (even for two-parent cases). No time limit on job search and job readiness (can count as long as the recipient is satisfactorily participating).	Any two-parent family that contains a parent exempt under the waiver will not be counted as a two-parent case for work participation purposes (not just in cases of disability, as in current law).
Delaware	9/30/02	Exempts a parent of a child under 13 weeks or if an adult is medically unable to participate. Individuals employed at least 30 hours per week are considered exempt.	If medically able to participate, adults may be required to participate part-time in parenting activities or other non-employment related activities regardless of the age of the youngest child. Allows unlimited job search. After two years of assistance, adult must participate in work experience for up to the number of hours equal to the cash welfare grant divided by the minimum wage. In addition, up to 10 additional hours of job search may be required.	
Hawaii	9/30/04	Exempts individuals who are ill or incapacitated for at least 30 days; providing in-home care for an ill or incapacitated assistance unit member; caring for an infant under six months; over age 60; or a VISTA volunteer.	Job search, education, and vocational education are not time-limited. Recipients who are not job ready are assigned to remediation to remove barriers. Recipients awaiting assignment to education or training activities may be assigned to up to 18 hours per week in temporary employment placements developed by employment specialists.	

State	Waiver Expiration Date	Exemptions	Activities/Hours	Other
Indiana	3/31/02	No waiver provision.	No minimum work hours. Individual is considered engaged in work if meeting the hours and activities in their individualized self-sufficiency plans. Allows education and training to count more than allowable under federal law.	
Kansas	9/30/03	No waiver provision.	Job search is not time-limited. Parents with a child under age six may be required to work more than 20 hours per week.	
Massachusetts	9/30/05	Exempts individuals who are single parents caring for a child under full-time school age (under three months if child is subject to family cap); disabled; needed in the home to care for a disabled family member; a pregnant woman beginning in her sixth month of pregnancy; ineligible persons unless they can legally work for pay; or aged 60 or over.	Requires 20 hours of work for each non-exempt adult (including each parent in a two-parent family). All work-related activities allowable under pre-1996 program count. No limits on number of hours in activities, and no time limit on job search.	
Minnesota	9/30/02	Exempts individuals who are age 60 or older; pregnant; providing care for a child under age one; experiencing a personal or family crisis; exempt under a domestic violence service plan; seriously ill, injured, or disabled; or needed in the home to care for another member of the household who is ill or disabled.	Any activity in individualized case plan counts (no preset list of activities; may include barrier removal or education). No limit on vocational education participation or on time in vocational education. Job search counts longer than allowed by federal law. Uses TANF hours rules.	If one parent in a two-parent case is exempt, the family will only be included when calculating the all-family work participation rate.

State	Waiver Expiration Date	Exemptions	Activities/Hours	Other
Missouri	6/30/00	No waiver provision.	Allows more educational activities: post-secondary education; General Educational Development Diploma (GED) testing; junior high school; high school; English as a Second Language (ESL); and Adult Basic Education (ABE), High School Equivalency, and/or Remedial Education. Uses TANF hours rules for single-parent cases. All two-parent families must participate 55 hours per week. Individuals in two-parent families may not count participation in post-secondary education, GED testing, high school, ESL, or ABE toward the first 30 hours.	
Montana	12/31/03	No exemptions from work participation.	All Demonstration pre-1996 welfare law activity hours count in participation totals. No time limit on job search. No limit on number of participants or time in educational activities (all hours count).	
Nebraska	6/30/03	Exempts caretaker relatives with a child under 12 weeks old.	No time limit on counting job search. All caretaker relative recipients are required to participate in some activity (education, job skills training, work experience, intensive job search, or employment activities). When a parent has a child between 12 weeks and six months old, only part-time participation in activities such as family nurturing is required. Family nurturing is counted as a JOBS activity. (However, participation in family nurturing will not count toward the calculation of the TANF participation rate.)	

State	Waiver Expiration Date	Exemptions	Activities/Hours	Other
New Hampshire	3/31/02	Retains all exemptions in effect 9/30/96. Also exempts parents when a child who would otherwise be subject to the family cap is born as a result of rape or incest (for children subject to family cap, 13 weeks); parents providing care for a child under age five (reduced to age three on 7/1/98); and individuals who have significant employment-related barriers (as defined in state policy manuals, individuals determined permanently incapable of self-sufficiency).	Allows unlimited job search. Requires 20 hours of work per week (in unsubsidized employment, subsidized job, On-the-Job Training (OJT), community service, work experience, work supplementation, or other approved work activity) for 26 weeks after 26 weeks of job search. Work activities may include post-secondary education, self-initiated education and training, and barrier resolution. Parents with children under age six may be required to participate more than 20 hours per week. Imposes time limits on education activities (time limit to be related to the average time it takes to complete a particular activity and to participant characteristics); after time limit, activity must be combined with work. Individuals without a high school diploma under age 21 required to participate in education. Noncustodial parents may be required to participate for up to 40 hours per week.	
Ohio	6/30/03	No waiver provision.	Recipients over age 21 without a high school diploma must be in education activities in order to remain eligible for benefits. Generally, recipients assigned to education activities have two years to complete high school, adult education, or GED, or they become ineligible for benefits.	Requires up-front job search while application is being processed.

State	Waiver Expiration Date	Exemptions	Activities/Hours	Other
Oregon	6/30/03	Oregon does not apply exemptions from work program participation. The following groups are exempt from sanction for failure to participate, but are counted in the numerator for Oregon's work participation calculation: VISTA volunteers; clients with unreasonable travel distance; clients in months seven and eight of pregnancy must only participate 10 hours per week; clients in their last month of pregnancy are deferred from participation through the first three months after birth; pregnant teens must participate in education or employment just like non-pregnant teens.	Case managers determine participation activities and hours for all recipients based on individual circumstances (may include ESL, substance abuse/mental health treatment).	
South Carolina	9/30/03	Exempts a pregnant adult from seventh month of pregnancy until birth; single-parent caring for a child under age one, unless the parent is under 25 and has not completed secondary school; incapacitated adults; an adult needed to care for an incapacitated individual; or an individual unable to participate because child care and/or reasonable transportation cannot be provided.	Job club/job search may last for up to 60 days; allows any educational activity below the post-secondary level that the state determines to be appropriate to the employment goal; participation in Family Life Skills can count. State does not apply TANF core activity requirements or restrictions on counting education.	
Tennessee	6/30/07	Exempts individuals who are disabled; caring for a disabled person; aged 60 or older; full-time VISTA volunteer, parent unable to obtain child care or transportation; parent with infant under 16 weeks of age; or determined to be severely limited due to physical, mental, or learning disability.	No time limit on countable job search. Counts self-employment and life skills training. Persons testing at grade levels 8.9 or below on a literacy test count by participation in adult basic education for at least 20 hours per week. Uses federal hours requirement.	
Texas	3/31/02	Exempts caretakers with children under the age of five, as of 9/1/96; under the age of four, as of 9/1/97; under the age of three, as of 1/1/00; under the age of two, as of 9/1/00; and under the age of one, as of 9/1/01.	Broader definition of work, including post-secondary education, no minimum hours in "core" activities; does not time limit job search.	

State	Waiver Expiration Date	Exemptions	Activities/Hours	Other
Utah	12/31/00	Requires participation of all AFDC parents and eligible children age 16 or older (if not in school)	Broader definition of work may include life skills components such as mental health treatment or addressing transportation issues; individual job search usually limited to 30 days; educational activities including ESL (not subject to the Family Employment Plan general 24-month educational limit); or post-secondary education. No minimum hours of participation; required hours are determined individually.	
Vermont	6/30/01	Requires pregnant and parenting minors to participate in education or training activities or parenting classes, even if they are in school full-time, working 30 hours per week, or needed in the home to care for an ill or incapacitated family member. Exempts needy non-parent caretakers.	No time limit on job search. Requires participation in community service jobs if unsubsidized employment is not found after 15 months for two-parent cases (40 hours per week) or after 30 months (20 hours per week or grant divided by minimum wage, whichever is less) for one-worker families with a child under age 13. If a family is working in unsubsidized employment, they can meet the work requirement with 75% of the hours required for community service. Parents with temporary disabilities who are deferred from participation in work activities must participate in rehabilitation and training programs. Requires a pregnant woman in second or third trimester of pregnancy to participate unless determined medically unable. Requires two-parent participants working more than 30 hours per week to participate in JOBS.	Non-exempt parents will be required to participate in job search in the two months before they are required to participate in the community jobs component.

State	Waiver Expiration Date	Exemptions	Activities/Hours	Other
Virginia	6/30/03	The following caretakers are exempt: minor caretakers under age 16; teen parents 16-19 who are in school or vocational or technical training full-time; individuals with a temporary medical condition, aged 60 or older, or needed in the home to care for an incapacitated family member; incapacitated individuals; parent caring for a child under 18 months of age; caretakers who are not the parents of the child; a woman in her fourth-ninth months of pregnancy.	Job search is required without time limits. Usually for 90 days, then assigned to work activity (subsidized employment or community service). Participants between 19 and 24 may be immediately assigned to work experience or education. Recipients who do not find unsubsidized employment may be required to participate in six-month subsidized employment placements.	

Source: Congressional Research Service (CRS,) based on information from the U.S. Department of Health and Human Services and TANF state plans.

Table A-5. Effect of Waivers on TANF Work Participation Rates: for States with Grandfathered Waivers: FY2000-FY2003

	2000			2001			2002			2003		
	With Waivers	Without Waivers	Differ-ence	With Waivers	Without Waivers	Differ-ence	With Waivers	Without Waivers	Differ-ence	With Waivers	Without Waivers	Differ-ence
Arizona	39.7%	39.%	0.0	32.9%	32.9%	0.0	25.9%	25.9%	0.0	NA	13.4%	NA
CT	43.0	33.2	9.8	40.6	27.6	13.0	NA	26.6	NA	NA	30.6	NA
Delaware	27.6	16.8	10.8	24.6	11.8	12.8	25.8	11.7	14.1	NA	18.2	NA
Hawaii	29.7	24.5	5.2	35.0	27.9	7.1	58.8	32.5	26.3	65.8	34.6	31.2
Indiana	72.3	40.8	31.5	76.0	43.3	32.7	62.6	45.3	17.3	NA	40.3	NA
Kansas	77.4	49.0	28.4	80.7	45.0	35.7	84.8	37.6	47.2	87.9	32.4	55.5
MA	69.2	7.1	62.1	76.5	10.9	65.6	60.9	9.2	51.7	61.0	8.4	52.6
Minnesota	34.7	29.3	5.4	35.2	28.3	6.9	40.4	31.2	9.2	NA	25.0	NA
Missouri	34.0	30.4	3.6	NA	33.1	NA	NA	25.4	NA	NA	28.0	NA
Montana	68.2	36.2	32.0	44.4	26.9	17.5	84.2	37.9	46.3	85.9	37.4	48.5
Nebraska	22.6	15.8	6.8	18.1	13.9	4.2	28.1	22.8	5.3	33.4	29.4	4.0
NH	53.1	30.0	23.1	50.2	29.9	20.3	41.8	32.6	9.2	NA	28.2	NA
Ohio	52.9	52.8	0.1	53.2	53.0	0.2	56.3	56.1	0.2	62.3	62.2	0.1
Oregon	64.0	10.6	53.4	72.0	11.1	60.9	61.1	8.0	53.1	60	14.7	45.3
South Carolina	54.0	25.0	29.0	58.7	32.0	26.7	52.4	30.2	22.2	54.3	28.6	25.7
Tennessee	35.4	24.9	10.5	32.3	20.8	11.5	41.2	14.3	26.9	42.7	13.4	29.3
Texas	25.6	7.8	17.8	41.5	15.6	25.9	30.8	21.1	9.7	NA	28.1	NA
Utah	31.1	27.9	3.2	25.9	25.0	0.9	NA	27.9	NA	NA	28.1	NA
Vermont	—	11.6	—	NA	12.9	NA	NA	21.4	NA	NA	24.3	NA
Virginia	44.9	24.6	20.3	44.3	22.7	21.6	42.9	22.6	20.3	44.6	29.9	14.7

Source: Congressional Research Service (CRS), based on data from the U.S. Department of Health and Human Services (HHS).

Notes: NA denotes "not applicable" because the grandfathered waiver expired. HHS did not compute a participation rate for Vermont in FY2000 based on its waiver.

Table A-6. Effect of Waivers on TANF Work Participation Rates: for States with Grandfathered Waivers: FY2004-FY2006

	2004			2005			2006		
	With Waivers	Without Waivers	Difference	With Waivers	Without Waivers	Difference	With Waivers	Without Waivers	Difference
Arizona	NA	25.5%	NA	NA	30.3%	NA	NA	29.6%	NA
Connecticut	NA	24.3	NA	NA	33.8	NA	NA	30.8	NA
Delaware	NA	22.1	NA	NA	22.6	NA	NA	25.3	NA
Hawaii	70.5	40.3	30.2	NA	35.5	NA	NA	37.3	NA
Indiana	NA	36.3	NA	NA	30.9	NA	NA	26.7	NA
Kansas	NA	88.0	NA	NA	86.7	NA	NA	77.2	NA
Massachusetts	60.0	10.3	49.7	59.9	12.6	47.3	NA	13.6	NA
Minnesota	NA	26.8	NA	NA	28.9	NA	NA	30.3	NA
Missouri	NA	19.5	NA	NA	20.0	NA	NA	18.7	NA
Montana	92.7	86.7	6.0	NA	83.1	NA	NA	79.2	NA
Nebraska	NA	34.5	NA	NA	31.8	NA	NA	32.0	NA
New Hampshire	NA	30.2	NA	NA	24.6	NA	NA	24.1	NA
Ohio	NA	65.2	NA	NA	58.3	NA	NA	54.9	NA
Oregon	NA	32.1	NA	NA	14.9	NA	NA	15.2	NA
South Carolina	NA	53.7	NA	NA	54.3	NA	NA	49.5	NA
Tennessee	50.6	13.0	37.6	52.1	14.3	37.8	57.2	16.8	40.4
Texas	NA	34.2	NA	NA	38.9	NA	NA	42.0	NA
Utah	NA	26.2	NA	NA	30.3	NA	NA	42.5	NA
Vermont	NA	24.9	NA	NA	22.4	NA	NA	22.2	NA
Virginia	NA	50.1	NA	NA	46.3	NA	NA	53.9	NA

Source: Congressional Research Service (CRS), based on data from the U.S. Department of Health and Human Services (HHS).

Notes: NA denotes not applicable because the grandfathered waiver expired.

Author Contact Information

Gene Falk
Specialist in Social Policy
gfalk@crs.loc.gov, 7-7344

www.ingramcontent.com/pod-product-compliance
Lightning Source LLC
Chambersburg PA
CBHW082202290526
45794CB00008B/3398